EMMANUEL JOSEPH

The Alchemy of Us, How Family, Creativity, and Community Turn Struggle into Strength

Copyright © 2025 by Emmanuel Joseph

All rights reserved. No part of this publication may be reproduced, stored or transmitted in any form or by any means, electronic, mechanical, photocopying, recording, scanning, or otherwise without written permission from the publisher. It is illegal to copy this book, post it to a website, or distribute it by any other means without permission.

First edition

*This book was professionally typeset on Reedsy.
Find out more at reedsy.com*

Contents

1. Chapter 1: The Foundation of Family — 1
2. Chapter 2: Creativity as a Lifeline — 3
3. Chapter 3: The Strength in Community — 5
4. Chapter 4: Nurturing Relationships — 7
5. Chapter 5: Embracing Vulnerability — 9
6. Chapter 6: The Role of Hope — 11
7. Chapter 7: The Power of Storytelling — 13
8. Chapter 8: Resilience Through Adaptability — 15
9. Chapter 9: The Gift of Perspective — 17
10. Chapter 10: The Influence of Culture — 19
11. Chapter 11: The Healing Power of Nature — 21
12. Chapter 12: Finding Strength in Adversity — 23
13. Chapter 13: The Role of Faith and Spirituality — 25
14. Chapter 14: The Importance of Self-Care — 27
15. Chapter 15: The Impact of Gratitude — 29
16. Chapter 16: The Role of Passion and Purpose — 31
17. Chapter 17: The Journey of Transformation — 33

1

Chapter 1: The Foundation of Family

Family is the bedrock of our lives. From the moment we are born, we are surrounded by the unconditional love and support of our family members. These bonds shape our identities and provide a sense of belonging that stays with us throughout our lives. Family is where we learn our first lessons about trust, compassion, and resilience. Through the ups and downs, the laughter and tears, our family members are there to offer a helping hand and a listening ear. Their unwavering presence gives us the courage to face life's challenges and the strength to overcome them.

The importance of family becomes even more apparent during difficult times. When we face adversity, it is our family that often provides the emotional support and encouragement we need to persevere. They remind us that we are not alone and that we can lean on each other for strength. This sense of solidarity fosters resilience and helps us navigate through the toughest of times. The shared experiences and collective memories create a bond that is unbreakable, reminding us that we are part of something greater than ourselves.

Family also plays a crucial role in shaping our values and beliefs. The lessons we learn from our parents, siblings, and extended family members influence our worldview and guide our actions. These values serve as a moral compass, helping us make decisions and navigate the complexities of life. The traditions and customs passed down through generations provide a sense of continuity and connection to our heritage. They remind us of our roots and the legacy we carry forward.

In addition to emotional and moral support, family often provides practical assistance during times of struggle. Whether it's financial help, childcare, or simply lending a hand with everyday tasks, family members are there to ease our burdens. This practical support can make a significant difference in our ability to cope with challenges and move forward. The acts of kindness and generosity within a family create a ripple effect, inspiring us to pay it forward and support others in our community.

2

Chapter 2: Creativity as a Lifeline

Creativity is a powerful tool that allows us to navigate through tough times. In moments of struggle, creative expression can serve as a lifeline, offering us a way to process our emotions and find solace. Whether it's through painting, writing, music, or any other form of creative activity, the act of creating can be deeply therapeutic. It provides an outlet for our feelings, allowing us to channel our pain, frustration, and hope into something tangible and meaningful.

For many, creativity becomes a refuge, a safe space where they can escape from the pressures and uncertainties of life. It allows us to tap into our inner worlds and explore the depths of our imagination. In this sanctuary of creativity, we can let our guard down and be our true selves. The process of creating something beautiful or meaningful can be incredibly empowering, giving us a sense of control and purpose when everything else feels chaotic.

Moreover, creativity has the power to transform our perspectives. When we engage in creative activities, we often find new ways of looking at our problems and challenges. It encourages us to think outside the box and consider alternative solutions. This shift in perspective can be invaluable in helping us navigate through difficult situations. By approaching our struggles with a creative mindset, we can uncover hidden strengths and possibilities that we may not have realized existed.

Creativity also fosters a sense of connection. Whether we share our creations with others or collaborate on a project, creative expression brings people together. It allows us to communicate and connect on a deeper level, transcending language and cultural barriers. The shared experience of creating and appreciating art builds a sense of community and solidarity, reminding us that we are not alone in our struggles.

3

Chapter 3: The Strength in Community

Community is where we find strength and resilience. In times of struggle, the support of our community can make all the difference. Whether it's a group of friends, neighbors, or a larger network of people who share common interests or values, our community provides a sense of belonging and solidarity. The relationships we build within our community offer emotional support, practical assistance, and a source of encouragement.

One of the most powerful aspects of community is the collective action it inspires. When people come together to address a common challenge or goal, they can achieve remarkable things. The combined efforts of individuals working towards a shared purpose create a synergy that amplifies their impact. This sense of collective empowerment can be incredibly motivating and uplifting, reminding us that we are stronger together.

Communities also provide a safety net during difficult times. When we face personal or collective crises, our community can step in to offer support and resources. This can include everything from financial assistance and access to essential services to emotional support and advocacy. The solidarity and compassion within a community create a sense of security and hope, helping us to weather the storms of life.

Moreover, the diversity within a community enriches our perspectives and experiences. By interacting with people from different backgrounds, cultures, and walks of life, we gain new insights and understanding. This diversity fosters a spirit of inclusivity and acceptance, encouraging us to embrace our differences and learn from one another. The strength of a community lies in its ability to bring people together and celebrate the richness of their collective experiences.

4

Chapter 4: Nurturing Relationships

Healthy relationships are essential for personal growth and well-being. The connections we form with others provide us with emotional support, encouragement, and a sense of purpose. Nurturing these relationships requires effort, communication, and mutual respect. Whether it's with family, friends, romantic partners, or colleagues, the bonds we cultivate play a significant role in our resilience and ability to navigate through life's challenges.

Friendships are particularly important in providing us with a sense of belonging and camaraderie. A strong friendship is built on trust, honesty, and shared experiences. Friends offer a listening ear, a shoulder to lean on, and a source of joy and laughter. They celebrate our successes and stand by us during difficult times. These meaningful connections remind us that we are valued and loved, helping us to stay grounded and resilient.

Romantic partnerships also contribute to our well-being and resilience. A healthy romantic relationship is characterized by mutual support, communication, and understanding. Partners who nurture each other's growth and provide emotional and practical support create a foundation of strength and stability. The intimacy and connection within a romantic relationship offer a sense of security and comfort, helping us to navigate through life's ups and downs.

Professional relationships, such as those with colleagues and mentors, are equally important. These connections provide opportunities for personal and career growth. A supportive work environment fosters collaboration, innovation, and a sense of purpose. Mentors offer guidance, wisdom, and encouragement, helping us to develop our skills and reach our potential. The relationships we build in our professional lives contribute to our overall resilience and success.

5

Chapter 5: Embracing Vulnerability

Vulnerability is often seen as a weakness, but it is actually a source of strength. Embracing vulnerability allows us to connect with others on a deeper level and fosters authenticity, empathy, and emotional resilience. When we allow ourselves to be vulnerable, we open up to the possibility of genuine connection and understanding. This willingness to be seen and heard in our most authentic selves is a powerful act of courage.

Vulnerability involves acknowledging our fears, insecurities, and imperfections. It means letting go of the need to appear strong and invulnerable at all times. By embracing our vulnerability, we give ourselves permission to be human and to experience the full range of emotions. This self-acceptance fosters a sense of compassion towards ourselves and others, creating a space for healing and growth.

Moreover, vulnerability is the foundation of meaningful relationships. When we allow ourselves to be vulnerable with others, we create an environment of trust and openness. This authenticity encourages others to share their own vulnerabilities, leading to deeper connections and mutual support. The bonds formed through shared vulnerability are resilient and enduring, providing a source of strength during difficult times.

Embracing vulnerability also enhances our emotional resilience. When we confront and process our emotions, we build the capacity to cope with life's challenges. Instead of suppressing or avoiding our feelings, we learn to navigate through them with grace and understanding. This emotional intelligence enables us to respond to adversity with resilience and adaptability, turning our struggles into opportunities for growth.

6

Chapter 6: The Role of Hope

Hope is a driving force that propels us forward in the face of adversity. It is an essential element of resilience, providing us with the motivation and optimism needed to endure difficult times. Hope is not just a passive feeling; it is an active choice to believe in the possibility of a better future. This belief gives us the strength to persevere and the courage to take action, even when the odds seem insurmountable.

The psychology of hope reveals its profound impact on our mental and emotional well-being. Research shows that individuals with higher levels of hope are more likely to set and achieve goals, cope with stress, and maintain a positive outlook on life. Hope fosters a sense of agency and control, empowering us to make meaningful changes in our lives. It encourages us to focus on solutions rather than problems, and to seek opportunities for growth and improvement.

Cultivating hope involves nurturing a positive mindset and focusing on what we can control. This can be achieved through practices such as setting realistic and achievable goals, visualizing success, and seeking support from others. Surrounding ourselves with positive influences and engaging in activities that bring us joy and fulfillment can also help sustain our sense of hope. By actively nurturing hope, we build a reservoir of inner strength that helps us navigate through life's challenges.

Hope is also a powerful force for collective resilience. In communities facing adversity, hope can inspire collective action and solidarity. It brings people together, fostering a sense of unity and shared purpose. The stories of individuals and communities overcoming hardship through hope and perseverance serve as powerful reminders of our capacity for resilience. By sharing these stories and supporting one another, we can create a culture of hope that empowers us all to thrive.

7

Chapter 7: The Power of Storytelling

Storytelling is a timeless tradition that connects us to our past, present, and future. It is a powerful means of communication that allows us to share our experiences, values, and wisdom. Through storytelling, we can make sense of our struggles and find meaning in our lives. It provides a platform for healing and empowerment, fostering empathy and understanding among individuals and communities.

The act of sharing our stories can be deeply therapeutic. It allows us to process our emotions, reflect on our experiences, and gain new insights. By giving voice to our struggles, we can release the burden of holding them inside and find relief in knowing that we are not alone. Storytelling also creates a sense of connection and solidarity, as others can relate to our experiences and offer support and encouragement.

Storytelling has the power to inspire change and transformation. Through compelling narratives, we can challenge stereotypes, break down barriers, and advocate for social justice. Stories of resilience and triumph in the face of adversity can serve as powerful motivators, encouraging others to persevere and pursue their dreams. By sharing these stories, we can amplify voices that may otherwise go unheard and create a more inclusive and compassionate society.

In addition to personal and social impact, storytelling enriches our cultural heritage. It preserves the wisdom and traditions of our ancestors, passing them down through generations. These stories provide a sense of continuity and connection to our roots, reminding us of the values and lessons that have shaped our identities. By keeping the art of storytelling alive, we honor our past and inspire future generations to carry forward the legacy of resilience and strength.

8

Chapter 8: Resilience Through Adaptability

Adaptability is a key component of resilience. It is the ability to adjust to changing circumstances and thrive in the face of uncertainty. Life is full of unpredictable events and challenges, and our capacity to adapt determines how well we navigate through them. Developing adaptability involves cultivating a mindset that embraces change, seeks solutions, and remains open to new possibilities.

A growth mindset is fundamental to adaptability. This mindset views challenges as opportunities for learning and growth rather than as obstacles. By approaching problems with curiosity and a willingness to learn, we can develop new skills and strategies to overcome them. This flexibility allows us to navigate through adversity with confidence and resilience, knowing that we have the capacity to adapt and thrive.

Embracing change is another crucial aspect of adaptability. Change can be unsettling and disruptive, but it is also a natural part of life. By accepting that change is inevitable, we can reduce our resistance to it and approach it with a proactive attitude. This involves letting go of rigid expectations and being open to new experiences and perspectives. Embracing change allows us to remain agile and responsive, making it easier to find solutions and opportunities in the face of adversity.

Finding creative solutions to problems is a hallmark of adaptability. When faced with challenges, thinking outside the box and exploring unconventional approaches can lead to innovative solutions. This creative problem-solving mindset encourages us to see possibilities where others may see limitations. By fostering creativity and adaptability, we build the resilience needed to navigate through life's uncertainties and emerge stronger on the other side.

9

Chapter 9: The Gift of Perspective

Perspective is a powerful tool that shapes our experiences and responses to adversity. The way we perceive and interpret events influences our emotions, thoughts, and actions. Cultivating a positive perspective can enhance our resilience and help us find meaning and hope in difficult situations. This involves shifting our focus from what we cannot control to what we can, and recognizing the opportunities for growth and learning that adversity presents.

One way to cultivate a positive perspective is through gratitude. Practicing gratitude involves acknowledging and appreciating the positive aspects of our lives, even in the midst of challenges. By focusing on what we are grateful for, we can shift our attention away from negativity and cultivate a sense of abundance and contentment. This positive outlook enhances our emotional well-being and strengthens our resilience.

Finding meaning in adversity is another important aspect of perspective. Difficult experiences can be valuable opportunities for growth and self-discovery. By reflecting on what we have learned from our struggles, we can gain new insights and a deeper understanding of ourselves and the world around us. This sense of meaning and purpose provides motivation and direction, helping us to navigate through challenges with resilience and determination.

Cultivating a positive perspective also involves challenging negative thought patterns and replacing them with more constructive ones. This requires self-awareness and mindfulness, allowing us to recognize when we are falling into negative thinking and consciously choose to shift our focus. By reframing our thoughts and focusing on solutions, possibilities, and strengths, we can create a more empowering and resilient mindset.

10

Chapter 10: The Influence of Culture

Culture plays a significant role in shaping our identities and resilience. It encompasses the values, traditions, and practices passed down through generations, providing us with a sense of belonging and continuity. Our cultural heritage serves as a source of strength and inspiration, helping us navigate through life's challenges. This chapter delves into the ways in which cultural values and practices contribute to our resilience and ability to overcome adversity.

Cultural values often emphasize the importance of community, family, and collective well-being. These values foster a sense of solidarity and mutual support, encouraging individuals to come together in times of need. Cultural practices such as communal gatherings, rituals, and celebrations create opportunities for connection and shared experiences. These traditions provide a sense of stability and continuity, reminding us of our roots and the collective strength of our community.

Additionally, cultural narratives and stories play a crucial role in shaping our resilience. Folktales, myths, and historical accounts often highlight themes of perseverance, courage, and triumph in the face of adversity. These stories serve as powerful reminders of our capacity to overcome challenges and inspire us to tap into our inner strength. By connecting with our cultural narratives, we gain a deeper understanding of our identity and the resilience that has been passed down through generations.

Cultural practices also provide us with coping mechanisms and strategies for dealing with stress and adversity. Traditional healing practices, mindfulness techniques, and artistic expressions are often rooted in cultural traditions. These practices offer valuable tools for managing emotions, finding balance, and fostering resilience. By integrating these cultural practices into our lives, we can enhance our well-being and strengthen our ability to navigate through difficult times.

11

Chapter 11: The Healing Power of Nature

Nature has a profound impact on our well-being and resilience. The natural world offers a sense of peace and tranquility, providing a refuge from the stresses of everyday life. This chapter explores the healing power of nature and how it helps us navigate through life's challenges. From the calming effects of being in natural environments to the therapeutic benefits of outdoor activities, we will discuss how nature can restore and rejuvenate our spirits.

Spending time in nature has been shown to reduce stress, anxiety, and depression. The sights, sounds, and smells of the natural world have a calming effect on our minds and bodies. Whether it's a walk in the park, a hike in the mountains, or simply sitting by the ocean, being in nature allows us to disconnect from the demands of modern life and reconnect with ourselves. This sense of calm and clarity enhances our emotional well-being and strengthens our resilience.

Engaging in outdoor activities also provides numerous physical and mental health benefits. Physical exercise, such as hiking, biking, or gardening, releases endorphins and improves our overall fitness. These activities also promote mindfulness and present-moment awareness, allowing us to fully engage with our surroundings and find joy in the simple pleasures of nature. The combination of physical movement and mindfulness fosters a sense of vitality and resilience.

Nature also offers valuable lessons in adaptability and resilience. The natural world is constantly changing and evolving, yet it remains resilient and thrives. By observing the cycles of nature, we can gain insights into our own capacity for growth and renewal. The changing seasons, the resilience of plants and animals, and the interconnectedness of ecosystems all remind us of the beauty and strength that emerge from life's challenges. Nature's resilience inspires us to embrace change and find strength in our own journey.

12

Chapter 12: Finding Strength in Adversity

Adversity is an inevitable part of life, but it also presents opportunities for growth and transformation. This chapter examines how we can find strength in adversity and emerge stronger on the other side. Through stories of resilience and perseverance, we will highlight the ways in which struggle can lead to personal and collective empowerment.

One of the key ways to find strength in adversity is by reframing challenges as opportunities for growth. This involves shifting our mindset from viewing adversity as a setback to seeing it as a catalyst for positive change. By embracing a growth mindset, we can approach challenges with curiosity and a willingness to learn. This perspective allows us to identify the lessons and opportunities for self-improvement that adversity presents.

Another important aspect of finding strength in adversity is building a support network. Surrounding ourselves with positive, supportive individuals can make a significant difference in our ability to cope with challenges. These relationships provide emotional support, practical assistance, and a sense of connection. By leaning on our support network, we can find the strength to persevere and overcome obstacles.

Adversity also fosters resilience by encouraging us to develop new skills and coping mechanisms. When faced with challenges, we are often pushed out of our comfort zones and forced to adapt. This process of adaptation strengthens our problem-solving abilities, emotional intelligence, and self-efficacy. By overcoming adversity, we build a reservoir of inner strength that we can draw upon in future challenges.

Finally, adversity can lead to a deeper sense of purpose and meaning in life. The struggles we face often prompt us to reflect on our values, priorities, and goals. This introspection can lead to a clearer understanding of what truly matters to us and inspire us to pursue our passions and dreams. By finding meaning in our struggles, we can transform adversity into a source of motivation and empowerment.

13

Chapter 13: The Role of Faith and Spirituality

Faith and spirituality provide a source of comfort and strength during difficult times. They offer a framework for understanding and navigating life's challenges, providing us with a sense of purpose and meaning. This chapter explores the role of faith and spirituality in building resilience and how spiritual practices and beliefs can support us in times of adversity.

Faith and spirituality often involve a belief in something greater than ourselves, whether it be a higher power, the universe, or a collective consciousness. This belief can provide a sense of hope and reassurance, reminding us that we are not alone in our struggles. The sense of connection to a higher power or greater purpose can offer comfort and guidance, helping us to navigate through difficult times with resilience and grace.

Spiritual practices, such as prayer, meditation, and mindfulness, are valuable tools for building resilience. These practices promote inner peace, emotional regulation, and a sense of grounding. By regularly engaging in spiritual practices, we can cultivate a deeper sense of self-awareness and connection to our inner wisdom. This inner strength enhances our ability to cope with stress and adversity, providing us with a stable foundation from which to navigate life's challenges.

Faith communities also play a significant role in building resilience. These communities provide a sense of belonging and support, offering a network of individuals who share similar beliefs and values. The relationships and connections within faith communities create a sense of solidarity and mutual support. During times of adversity, faith communities often come together to offer practical assistance, emotional support, and collective prayer or meditation. This collective strength and compassion foster resilience and help individuals and communities navigate through difficult times.

14

Chapter 14: The Importance of Self-Care

Self-care is essential for maintaining our physical, emotional, and mental well-being. It involves taking deliberate actions to nurture and care for ourselves, especially during times of stress and adversity. This chapter focuses on the importance of self-care and how it contributes to our resilience. We will explore various self-care practices and discuss how prioritizing self-care can help us navigate through life's challenges with greater ease and strength.

Self-care is not a one-size-fits-all approach; it is highly individualized and can take many forms. For some, self-care may involve physical activities such as exercise, yoga, or taking walks in nature. These activities promote physical health, release endorphins, and provide a sense of vitality. For others, self-care may involve creative pursuits such as painting, writing, or playing a musical instrument. Engaging in creative activities allows us to express ourselves, find joy, and reduce stress.

Emotional self-care is equally important and involves practices that help us process and manage our emotions. This can include activities such as journaling, talking to a trusted friend or therapist, or practicing mindfulness and meditation. These practices allow us to reflect on our feelings, gain insights, and cultivate a sense of inner calm. By tending to our emotional well-being, we build the resilience needed to cope with life's challenges.

In addition to physical and emotional self-care, mental self-care involves activities that stimulate our minds and foster personal growth. This can include reading, learning new skills, solving puzzles, or engaging in meaningful conversations. Mental self-care keeps our minds sharp, enhances our problem-solving abilities, and provides a sense of accomplishment. By incorporating self-care into our daily lives, we create a strong foundation for resilience and well-being.

15

Chapter 15: The Impact of Gratitude

Gratitude is a powerful emotion that enhances our resilience and overall well-being. It involves recognizing and appreciating the positive aspects of our lives, even in the midst of challenges. This chapter delves into the impact of gratitude and how it helps us cope with adversity. We will discuss the science behind gratitude, its benefits, and practical ways to cultivate a grateful mindset in our daily lives.

Research has shown that practicing gratitude has numerous psychological and physical benefits. Gratitude enhances our mood, reduces stress, and improves our mental health. It shifts our focus from what is lacking to what is abundant, fostering a sense of contentment and fulfillment. By regularly acknowledging and appreciating the positive aspects of our lives, we can cultivate a more optimistic and resilient mindset.

One of the most effective ways to practice gratitude is through journaling. Writing down the things we are grateful for each day helps us to reflect on and appreciate the positive moments and experiences. This practice reinforces a positive outlook and encourages us to focus on the good in our lives. Additionally, expressing gratitude to others, whether through words or actions, strengthens our relationships and fosters a sense of connection.

Gratitude also involves appreciating the small, everyday moments that bring us joy. It encourages us to be present and mindful, savoring the simple pleasures of life. Whether it's enjoying a cup of tea, watching a beautiful sunset, or spending time with loved ones, these moments of gratitude enhance our well-being and resilience. By cultivating a grateful mindset, we can find strength and positivity even in challenging times.

Practicing gratitude does not mean ignoring or minimizing the difficulties we face. Instead, it involves acknowledging both the challenges and the blessings in our lives. This balanced perspective allows us to approach adversity with a sense of hope and resilience. By embracing gratitude, we can navigate through life's challenges with a deeper sense of appreciation and inner strength.

16

Chapter 16: The Role of Passion and Purpose

Passion and purpose provide a sense of direction and motivation in our lives. They are the driving forces that inspire us to pursue our dreams and overcome obstacles. This chapter examines the importance of pursuing our passions and finding our purpose as a means of building resilience. Through inspiring stories and practical insights, we will explore how aligning our actions with our values and passions can help us navigate through challenges and thrive.

Passion is the enthusiasm and excitement we feel for the activities and pursuits that bring us joy and fulfillment. It fuels our creativity, determination, and perseverance. When we are passionate about something, we are more likely to invest time and effort into it, even when faced with challenges. Pursuing our passions provides a sense of purpose and meaning, making it easier to navigate through difficulties and setbacks.

Purpose is the sense of meaning and direction that guides our lives. It is the larger vision that inspires us to make a positive impact on the world. Finding our purpose involves reflecting on our values, strengths, and the contributions we want to make. When we align our actions with our purpose, we experience a deeper sense of fulfillment and resilience. Purpose provides a sense of motivation and determination, helping us to stay focused and driven even in the face of adversity.

To discover our passions and purpose, it is important to explore different interests and activities. This involves being open to new experiences, taking risks, and following our curiosity. By trying out various pursuits, we can identify what truly resonates with us and brings us joy. Reflecting on our values and the impact we want to make can also provide insights into our purpose. This self-discovery process allows us to align our actions with our passions and create a meaningful and fulfilling life.

Pursuing our passions and purpose is not always easy, and it may involve overcoming obstacles and setbacks. However, the sense of fulfillment and resilience that comes from living in alignment with our true selves makes the journey worthwhile. By staying true to our passions and purpose, we can navigate through life's challenges with confidence, determination, and a sense of meaning.

17

Chapter 17: The Journey of Transformation

The journey of transformation is a continuous process of growth and self-discovery. It involves embracing change, learning from our experiences, and evolving into our best selves. This final chapter reflects on the themes of family, creativity, and community as catalysts for turning struggle into strength. We will celebrate the resilience and courage that emerge from our challenges and discuss how we can continue to evolve and thrive on our journey of transformation.

Transformation often begins with a willingness to change and grow. This involves letting go of old habits, beliefs, and patterns that no longer serve us. By embracing a mindset of continuous improvement, we open ourselves up to new possibilities and opportunities for growth. This willingness to evolve allows us to adapt to changing circumstances and find strength in our journey.

Family, creativity, and community play integral roles in our transformation. The support and love of our family provide a stable foundation from which we can grow. Creativity allows us to explore new ideas, express ourselves, and find innovative solutions to challenges. Community offers a sense of belonging and solidarity, reminding us that we are not alone in our journey. These elements work together to empower us and foster our resilience.

The journey of transformation is not always linear, and it often involves setbacks and obstacles. However, these challenges are valuable opportunities for learning and growth. By reflecting on our experiences and embracing the lessons they offer, we can continue to evolve and become stronger. The process of transformation is a testament to our resilience and ability to overcome adversity.

As we continue on our journey of transformation, it is important to stay true to our values and passions. By aligning our actions with our purpose, we can create a meaningful and fulfilling life. The journey of transformation is a celebration of our resilience, courage, and capacity for growth. It is a reminder that through family, creativity, and community, we can turn struggle into strength and thrive in the face of adversity.

Book Description:

In "The Alchemy of Us," discover a transformative journey that reveals how the pillars of family, creativity, and community turn life's struggles into sources of incredible strength. This insightful book delves deep into the essence of resilience, illustrating how our closest bonds, artistic expressions, and collective efforts help us navigate through the toughest of times.

Drawing from rich anecdotes and profound wisdom, "The Alchemy of Us" explores the crucial role of family as the unwavering foundation of our lives. It emphasizes how the love and support of our loved ones provide the courage and stability to overcome challenges and foster personal growth.

The book also highlights the power of creativity as a lifeline, showcasing how engaging in artistic pursuits and imaginative thinking can offer solace and inspire new perspectives. Through creative expression, we can process emotions, find joy, and discover innovative solutions to our problems.

Furthermore, "The Alchemy of Us" examines the strength found within our communities. It celebrates the collective resilience that emerges when individuals come together to support one another. The stories of solidarity and mutual aid demonstrate how communities can uplift and empower us, creating a sense of belonging and shared purpose.

With each chapter, readers will gain a deeper understanding of how embracing vulnerability, nurturing relationships, and cultivating hope can

CHAPTER 17: THE JOURNEY OF TRANSFORMATION

enhance our resilience. The book also explores the impact of cultural heritage, the healing power of nature, and the significance of gratitude, faith, and self-care in building a life of strength and fulfillment.

"The Alchemy of Us" is an inspiring testament to the human spirit, offering valuable insights and practical strategies for turning struggle into strength. It is a celebration of the enduring power of family, creativity, and community in helping us thrive and transform our lives.

www.ingramcontent.com/pod-product-compliance
Lightning Source LLC
LaVergne TN
LVHW010441070526
838199LV00066B/6129